Gigi Hadid Adult Coloring Book

Zayn's Ex Girlfriend and Hot Top Model, Sexy Persona and Vogue Angel Inspired Adult Coloring Book

Heather Nelson

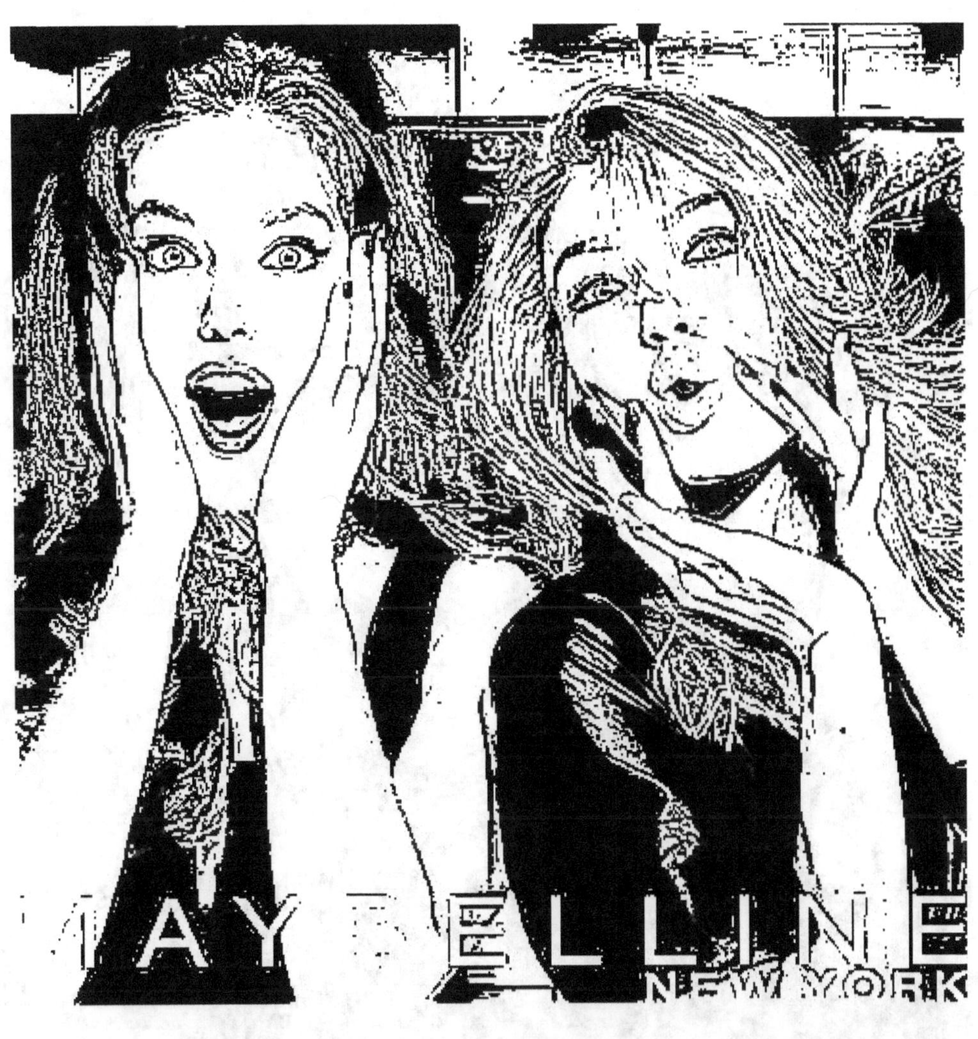

AY ELLINE
NEW YORK

MAYBELLINE
NEW YORK

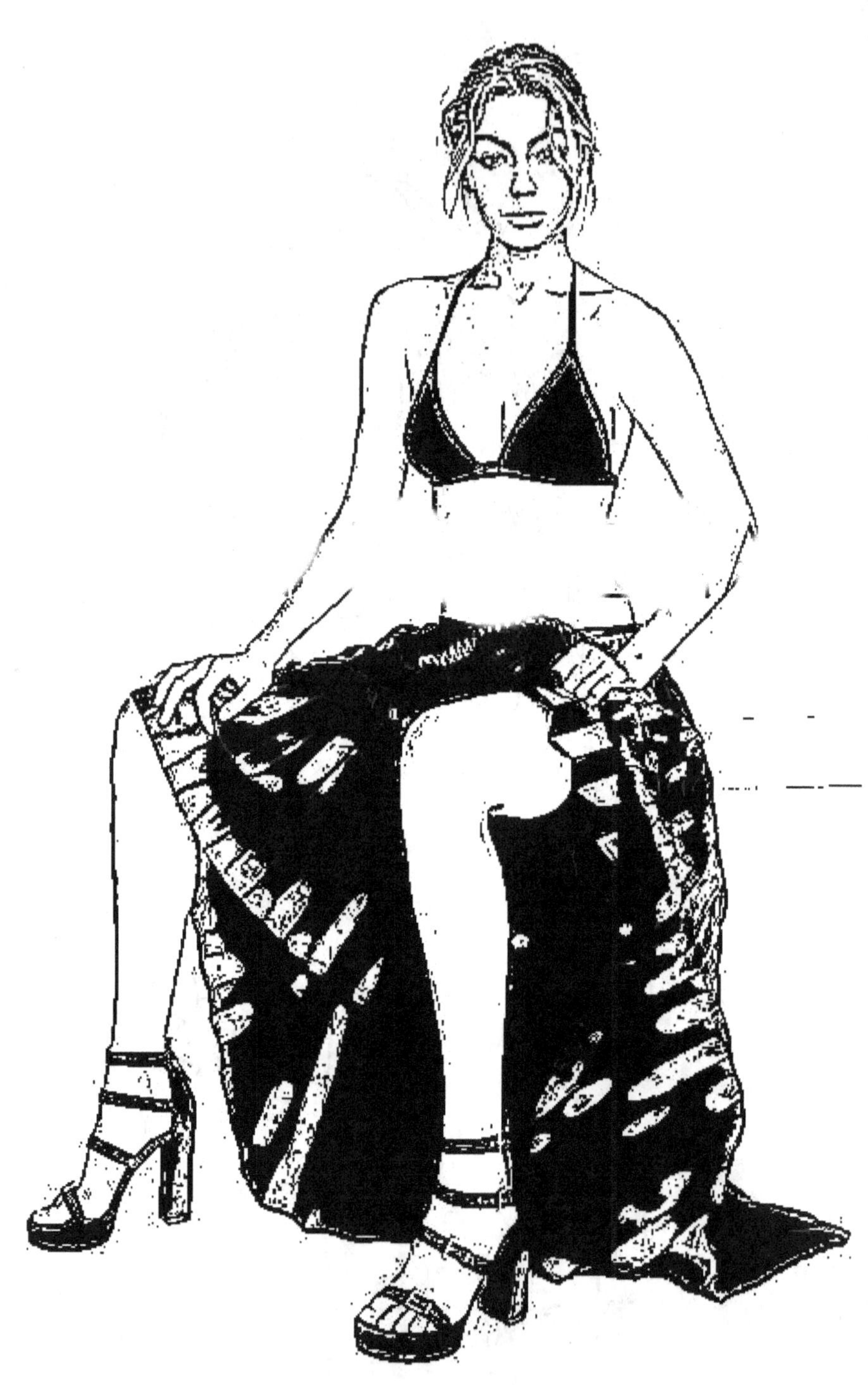

VOGUE
PARIS
Mars N°963
Mode :
LE STYLE
N'A
PLUS
DE
TABOU.
Isabelle
Huppert
Message
personnel.
LES
SECRETS
DE
Zoolander.
Gigi Hadid
LE
CORPS
phénomène
aux
10 millions
de fans.

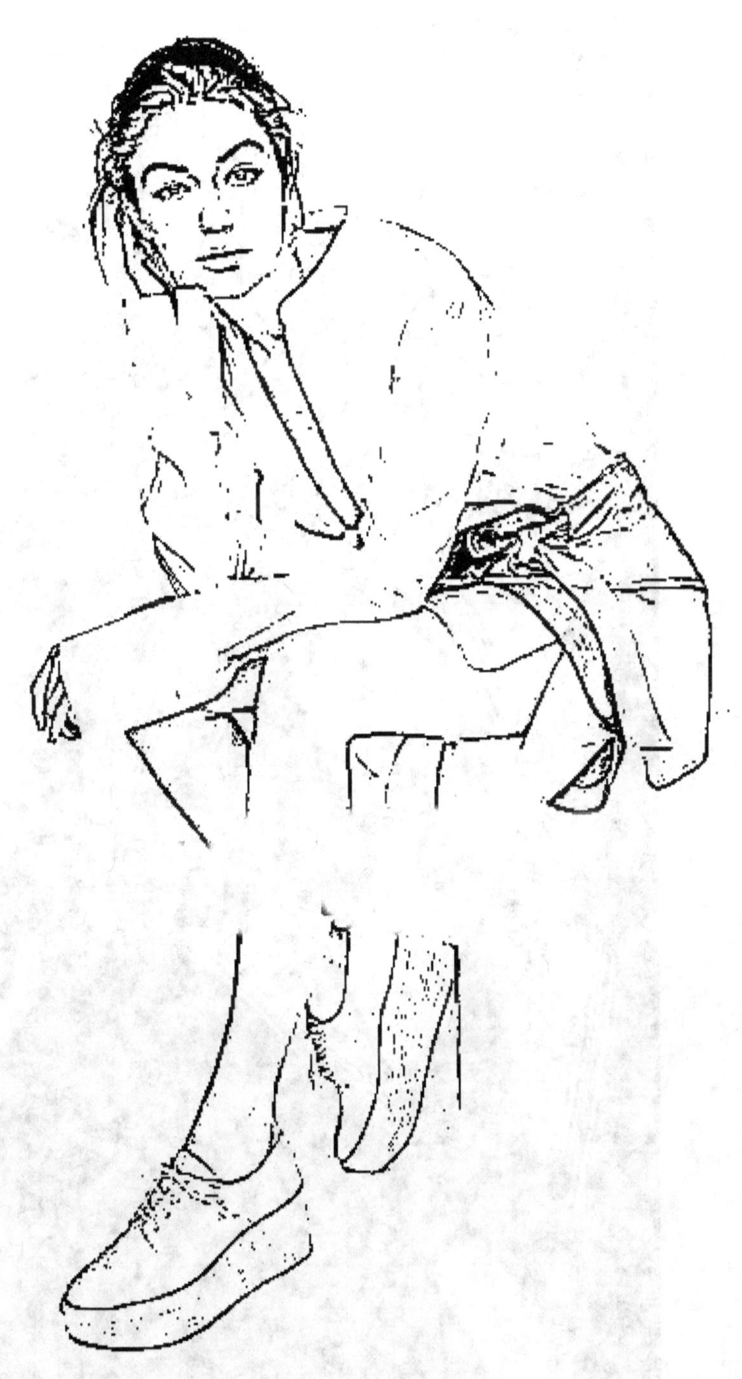

RONC

BALDININI
BAL
BAL

CATI
BEVERLY HILLS